Widdecombe Fair

Illustrated by Christine Price

Widdecombe Fair

An Old English Folk Song

FREDERICK WARNE & CO., INC.
NEW YORK AND LONDON

U. S. 1457264

To the Rampone Family
on the Price Farm

"Tom Pearse, Tom Pearse,
lend me your grey mare,

All along down along out along lee,
For I want for to go to Widdecombe Fair,

Wi' Bill Brewer, Jan Stewer, Peter Gurney, Peter Davy,

Dan'l Whiddon, Harry Hawk, old Uncle Tom Cobbleigh and all."
Old Uncle Tom Cobbleigh and all.

"And when shall I see again my grey mare?
All along down along out along lee,

"By Friday soon, or Saturday noon,

Wi' Bill Brewer, Jan Stewer,

Peter Gurney, Peter Davy,

Dan'l Whiddon, Harry Hawk,

old Uncle Tom Cobbleigh and all."

Old Uncle Tom Cobbleigh and all.

Then Friday came, and Saturday noon,
All along down along out along lee,

But Tom Pearse's old mare hath not trotted home,
  Wi' Bill Brewer, Jan Stewer,
    Peter Gurney, Peter Davy, Dan'l Whiddon,

Harry Hawk, old Uncle Tom Cobbleigh and all.
Old Uncle Tom Cobbleigh and all.

So Tom Pearse he got up to the top o' the hill
All along down along out along lee,

And he seed his old mare down a-making her will

Wi' Bill Brewer, Jan Stewer,

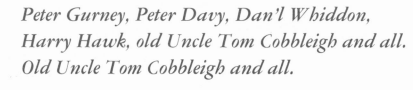

Peter Gurney, Peter Davy, Dan'l Whiddon,
Harry Hawk, old Uncle Tom Cobbleigh and all.
Old Uncle Tom Cobbleigh and all.

So Tom Pearse's old mare, her took sick and died.
All along down along out along lee,

*And Tom he sat down
on a stone, and he cried*

Wi' Bill Brewer, Jan Stewer,
Peter Gurney, Peter Davy,
Dan'l Whiddon, Harry Hawk,
old Uncle Tom Cobbleigh and all.
Old Uncle Tom Cobbleigh and all.

When the wind whistles cold on the moor of a night
All along down along out along lee,

Tom Pearse's old mare doth appear, gashly white,

Wi' Bill Brewer, Jan Stewer, Peter Gurney, Peter Davy,

Dan'l Whiddon, Harry Hawk,

old Uncle Tom Cobbleigh and all.

Old Uncle Tom Cobbleigh and all.

And all the long night be heard skirling and groans,
All along down along out along lee,
From Tom Pearse's old mare in her rattling bones,

And from Bill Brewer, Jan Stewer, Peter Gurney, Peter Davy,

Dan'l Whiddon, Harry Hawk, old Uncle Tom Cobbleigh and all,

Old Uncle Tom Cobbleigh and all.

The Music of WIDDECOMBE FAIR
and a Word about the Song.

WIDDECOMBE FAIR is a folk song, one of the best-known and best-loved of old English songs. English children grow up singing it, in and out of school, and even people who know no other folk songs will gladly sing about "Uncle Tom Cobbleigh and all."

Few of them realize that Uncle Tom Cobbleigh was a real person! He lived and died nearly two hundred years ago in the county of Devonshire in the West of England, not far from the village of Widecombe-on-the-Moor, where the song comes from. It was there, perhaps in the village inn at the time of the famous Fair, that someone first sang of Tom Pearse's old mare to a lusty old Devonshire tune.

In those days, the Fair was a big event, happening in September, when the village would be thronged with people, come to buy and sell and enjoy the fun. Many had to travel far to Widecombe over the moor—wild and lonely country, the haunt of goblins, ghosts and fairies. Even today, strange things can happen on the moor, especially on stormy nights, as anyone can tell from the story of WIDDECOMBE FAIR!

Tom Pearse Tom Pearse lend me your grey mare All a-long down a-long

out a-long lee, For I want for to go to Wid-de-combe Fair with Bill Brewer, Jan Stewer, Peter

Gurney, Peter Davy, Dan'l Whiddon, Harry Hawk, old un – cle Tom Cobbleigh and

all _____ old un – cle Tom Cobbleigh and all.